I0813986

Intro to Japanese

Bela Davis

にほんご
ni•ho•n•go

Abdo Kids Junior
is an Imprint of Abdo Kids
abdobooks.com

Abdo
INTRO TO LANGUAGE
Kids

Published by Abdo Kids, a division of ABDO, P.O. Box 398166, Minneapolis, Minnesota 55439.

Printed in the United States of America, North Mankato, Minnesota.

102023

012024

Consultant: Nao Yamanishi

Photo Credits: Getty Images, Shutterstock

Production Contributors: Teddy Borth, Jennie Forsberg, Grace Hansen

Design Contributors: Candice Keimig, Colleen McLaren

Publisher's Cataloging-in-Publication Data

Names: Davis, Bela, author.

Title: Intro to Japanese / by Bela Davis

Description: Minneapolis, Minnesota : Abdo Kids, 2024 | Series: Intro to language | Includes online resources and index.

Identifiers: ISBN 9781098268329 (lib. bdg.) | ISBN 9781098269029 (ebook) | ISBN 9781098269371 (Read-to-Me ebook)

Subjects: LCSH: Japanese language--Juvenile literature. | Informal language learning--Juvenile literature. | Language and languages--Juvenile literature. | Bilingual books--Juvenile literature.

Classification: DDC 418.00--dc23

Table of Contents

Intro to Japanese ... 4

Numbers ... 6

Colors ... 10

Greetings ... 12

Family ... 16

Animals ... 20

Places ... 22

Hiragana ... 23

Index ... 24

Abdo Kids Code ... 24

Intro to Japanese

Japanese is the language of Japan. Let's learn some words!

(Guide to letter sounds on page 23)

N
W
E
S
Asia
Japan
Pacific
Ocean

いち
i•chi
one
に
ni
two
ろく
ro•ku
six
なな
na•na
seven

さん
san
three

し
shi
four

ご
go
five

はち
ha•chi
eight

きゅう
kyū
nine

じゅう
jū
ten

じゅういち
jū•i•chi
eleven

じゅうに
jū•ni
twelve

じゅうろく
jū•ro•ku
sixteen

じゅうなな
jū•na•na
seventeen

じゅうさん
jū•san
thirteen

じゅうし
jū•shi
fourteen

じゅうご
jū•go
fifteen

じゅうはち
jū•ha•chi
eighteen

じゅうきゅう
jū•kyū
nineteen

にじゅう
ni•jū
twenty

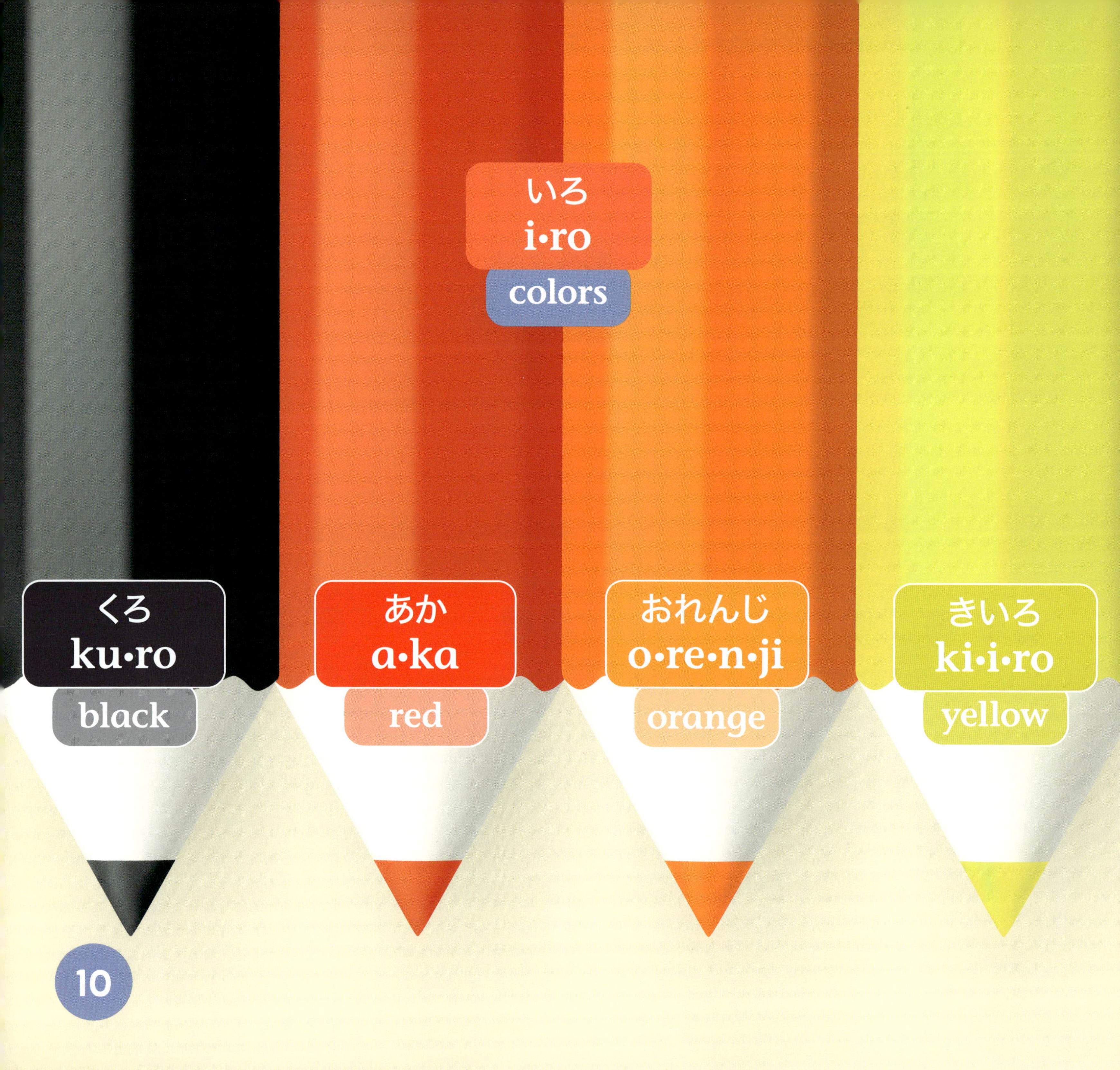
いろ
i•ro
colors
くろ
ku•ro
black
あか
a•ka
red
おれんじ
o•re•n•ji
orange
きいろ
ki•i•ro
yellow

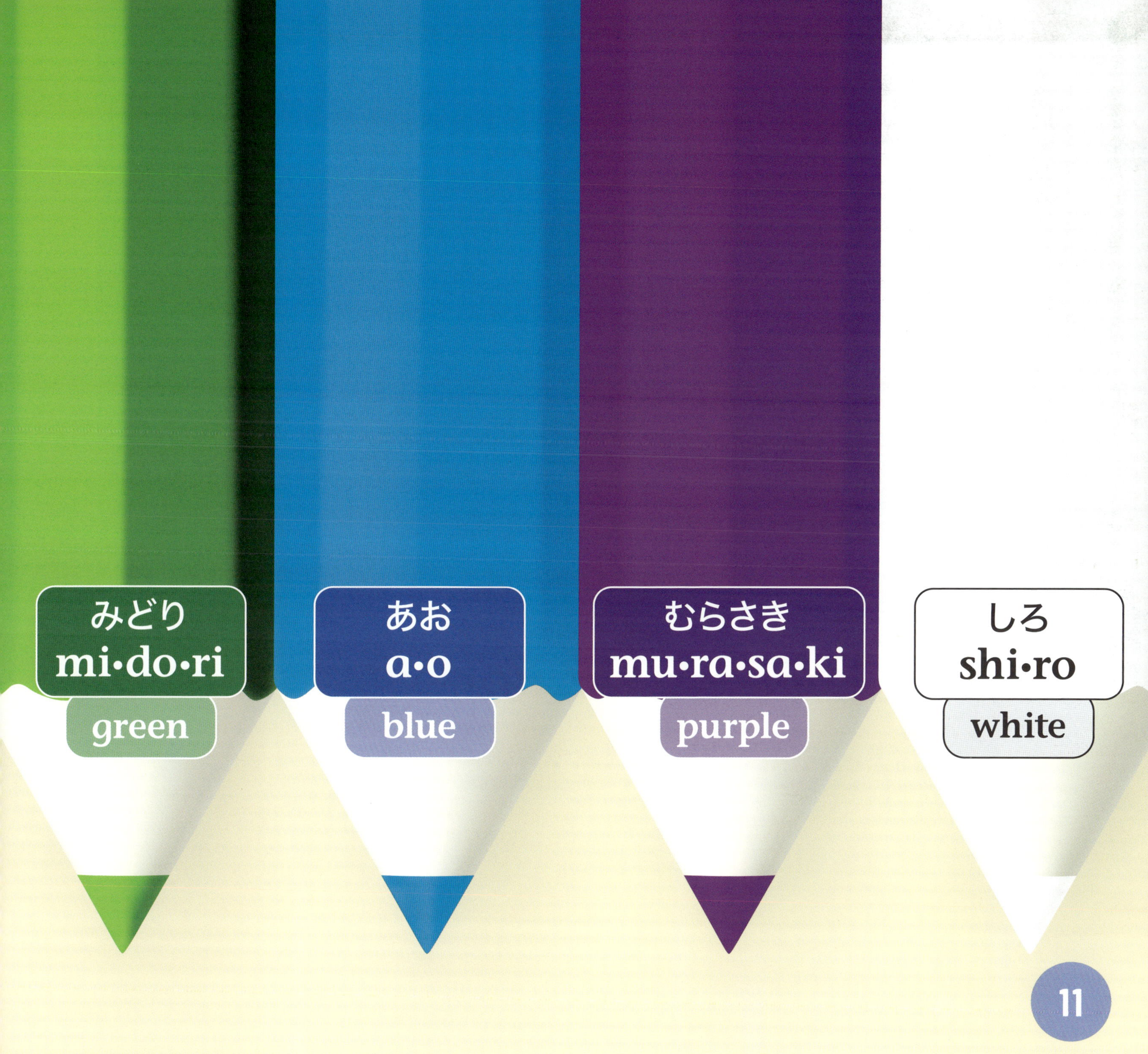
みどり
mi•do•ri
green
あお
a•o
blue
むらさき
mu•ra•sa•ki
purple
しろ
shi•ro
white

こんにちは
ko•n•ni•chi•wa
hello

さようなら
sa•yō•na•ra
goodbye

おはよう
o•ha•yō
good morning

おやすみ
o•ya•su•mi
good night

2.10

おねがいします
o•ne•ga•i•shi•ma•su
please

ありがとう
a•ri•ga•tō
thank you

はい
ha•i
yes

いいえ
ii•e
no

LEMONADE
LEMONADE
50 ¢

おかあさん
o•kaa•sa•n
mom

おとうさん
o•tō•sa•n
dad

いもうと
i•mō•to
younger sister

おとうと
o•tō•to
younger brother

おねえちゃん
o•ne•e•cha•n
older sister

おにいちゃん
o•ni•i•cha•n
older brother

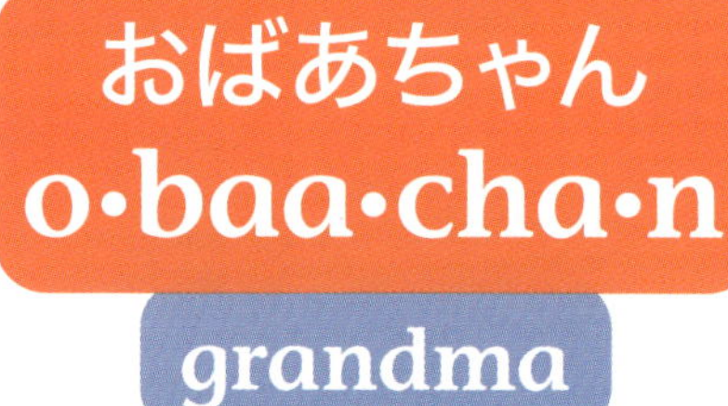

おばあちゃん
o•baa•cha•n
grandma

おじいちゃん
o•jii•cha•n
grandpa

おばちゃん
o•ba•cha•n
aunt

おじちゃん
o•ji•cha•n
uncle

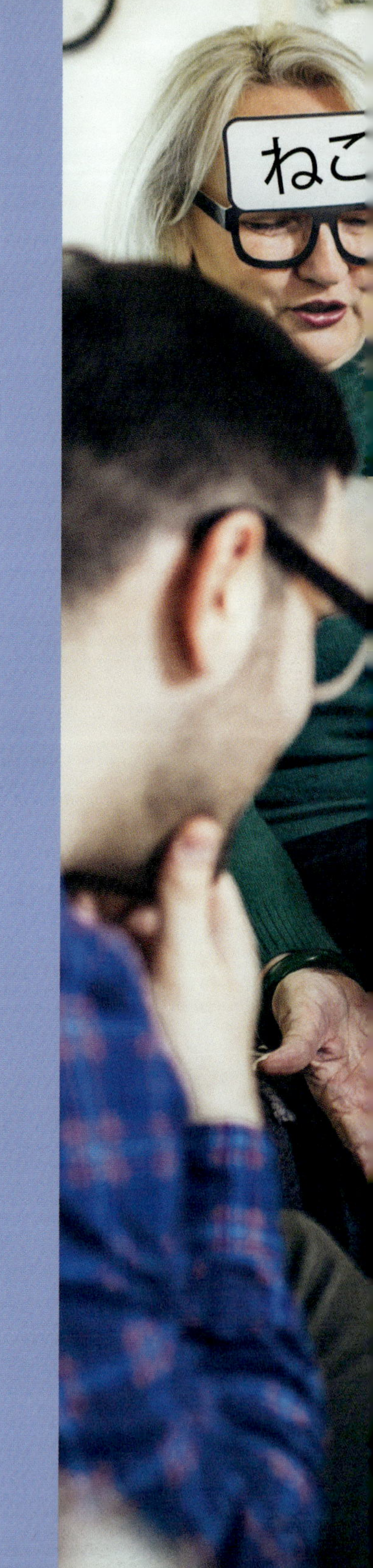

とり
さかな
やぎ
いぬ

どうぶつ
dō•bu•tsu
animals
いぬ
i•nu
dog
ねこ
ne•ko
cat

とり
to•ri
bird
サカナ
sa•ka•na
fish

ばしょ ba•sho – Places

いえ
i•e
house

がっこう
gak•ko
school

こうえん
ko•e•n
park

すなはま
su•na•ha•ma
sandy beach

letter
sound

あ a ah	は ha hah	か ka kah	ま ma mah	な na nah	ら ra rah	さ sa sah	た ta tah	や ya yah
い i ee	ひ hi hee	き ki kee	み mi mee	に ni nee	り ri ree	し shi she	ち chi chee	
う u oo	ふ hu who	く ku koo	む mu moo	ぬ nu new	る ru rew	す su sue	つ tsu tsue	ゆ yu you
え e ayy	へ he hay	け ke kay	め me may	ね ne nay	れ re ray	せ se say	て te tay	
お o oh	ほ ho hoh	こ ko koh	も mo moh	の no no	ろ ro row	そ so so	と to toh	よ yo yo
						わ wa wah	を wo oh	ん n nn

ひらがな
Hiragana

Index

animals 20-21

colors 10-11

family 16, 18

goodbyes 12

greetings 12

numbers 6-9

pleasantries 14

Visit **abdokids.com** to access crafts, games, videos, and more!

Use Abdo Kids code

IIK8329

or scan this QR code!